STEM IN SPORTS:
SCIENCE

SCIENCE   TECHNOLOGY   ENGINEERING   MATH

THE STEM IN SPORTS SERIES

STEM in Sports: Science, by Jim Gigliotti

STEM in Sports: Technology, by James Buckley, Jr.

STEM in Sports: Engineering, by Tim Newcomb

STEM in Sports: Math, by James Buckley Jr.

STEM IN SPORTS:
SCIENCE

by Jim Gigliotti

Mason Crest
450 Parkway Drive, Suite D
Broomall, PA 19008
www.masoncrest.com

@ 2015 by Mason Crest, an imprint of National Highlights, Inc.

Printed and bound in the United States of America.

Series ISBN: 978-1-4222-3230-9
Hardback ISBN: 978-1-4222-3233-0
EBook ISBN: 978-1-4222-8677-7

First printing
1 3 5 7 9 8 6 4 2

Produced by Shoreline Publishing Group LLC
Santa Barbara, California
Editorial Director: James Buckley Jr.
Designer: Patty Kelley
www.shorelinepublishing.com

Library of Congress Cataloging-in-Publication Data is on file with the publisher.

CONTENTS

KEY ICONS TO LOOK FOR:

Words to Understand: These words with their easy-to-understand definitions will increase the reader's understanding of the text, while building vocabulary skills.

Sidebars: This boxed material within the main text allows readers to build knowledge, gain insights, explore possibilities, and broaden their perspectives by weaving together additional information to provide realistic and holistic perspectives.

Research Projects: Readers are pointed toward area of further inquiry connected to each chapter. Suggestions are provided for projects that encourage deeper research and analysis.

Text-Dependent Questions: These questions send the reader back to the text for more careful attention to the evidence presented here.

Series Glossary of Key Terms: This back-of-the-book glossary contains terminology used throughout this series. Words found here increase the reader's ability to read and comprehend higher-level books and articles in this field.

INTRODUCTION

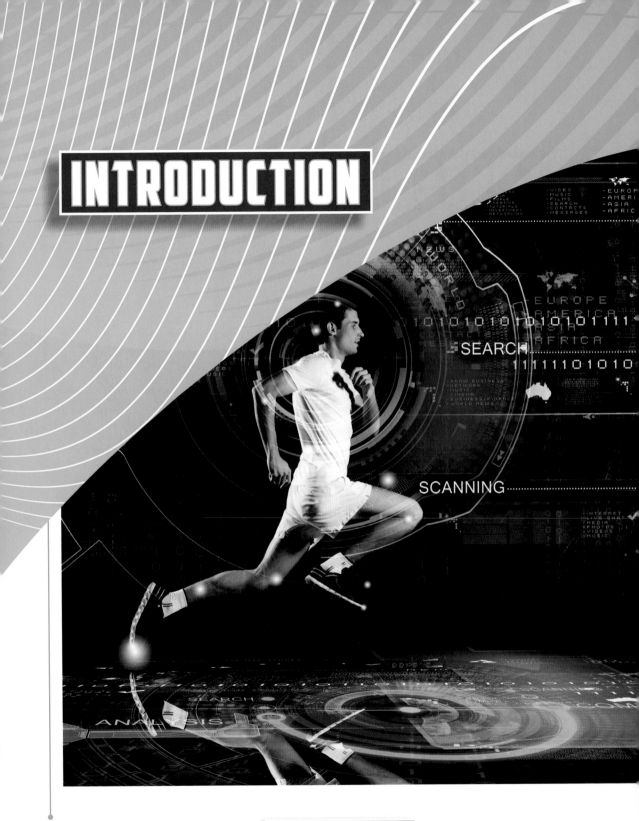

STEM IS THE HOTTEST BUZZWORD IN education. The letters stand for Science, Technology, Engineering, and Math. Those areas of study and work will be at the forefront of business, education, careers, and life for the coming decades. More jobs are opening up in those fields than in any other areas. But as this series shows, STEM is more than just programming computers or designing new apps. The concepts of STEM cross over into just about every area of life. In this series, we focus on how STEM is impacting the world of sports.

This volume focuses on Science. What is science? A dictionary calls science "knowledge derived from observation, study, and experimentation in order to determine the nature or principles of what is being studied." That definition covers more ground than Mike Trout does in center field! And it leaves as much open to question as soccer's offside law.

In sports, science touches on medicine, nutrition, strength and conditioning, performance analysis, and much more. Each individual part of STEM works hand-in-hand with the others, but science seals the deal.

CHAPTER 1

ATHLETES

FOR AS LONG AS SPORTS HAVE BEEN AROUND, fans and experts have wondered: What makes a great athlete? Is he or she born with all that talent? Or is it a matter of "practice makes perfect"? In his 2008 best-selling book, *Outliers: The Story of Success*, Canadian journalist Malcolm Gladwell suggested the "10,000-Hour Rule." He said that it worked for any field—business, the arts, or sports. The rule simply means that working at a task for 10,000 hours over the course of a lifetime leads to success. For instance, Gladwell believes that he is a successful author because he spent more than 10,000 hours working on stories for newspapers

How many more hours will this player need before he has "mastered" his skills?

and magazines. The Beatles became a great rock-and-roll band because they spent more than 10,000 hours in the recording studio, onstage, or somewhere playing music. And any elite athlete has easily gone over 10,000 hours playing and practicing by the time he reaches the top level of his sport.

Gladwell's 10,000-Hour Rule was actually based on the findings of a study by Anders Ericsson. Ericsson was a Swedish-born psychologist who found that elite performers in areas such as chess and sports got that way through extended, targeted practice. Coaches have been saying that for decades, but science proved it.

Like all scientific studies, Ericsson's findings employed the scientific method. The scientific method is a step-by-step process from observation to conclusion (see box at right).

The Quickest Way to First Base

LET'S APPLY THE SCIENTIFIC METHOD TO THE WORLD of sports. For instance, one question baseball fans ask: Is it better to dive into first base on a close play, or to run through the bag? As baseball fans can tell you, more often than not, the batter will run through first base. But when the batter dives into the bag, announcers and fans are quick to say that the player used extra hustle. "That guy will do anything to help his team!" they'll

WORDS TO UNDERSTAND

hacker in this case, slang for an unskilled golfer.

hypothesis a proposed solution based on limited evidence.

prosthetics devices that replace a missing human limb

rehabilitation the process of returning to full physical ability through exercise

torque the turning force on an object that produces the movement of rotation.

Quick Look: The Scientific Method

Here's something you've probably seen in science class—but it's always good to review! The five steps in the scientific method are observation, hypothesis, prediction, experiment, and conclusion.

1. A scientist observes something and does as much research as possible before she . . .

2. Develops a **hypothesis**, or general theory about what she thinks about the phenomena, which allows her to make a . . .

3. Specific prediction about what she will be able to prove by an . . .

4. Experiment that is properly and fairly designed to test her hypothesis and arrive at a . . .

5. Conclusion about whether the hypothesis should be accepted or rejected.

say. But is diving really a better way to get on base? The hypothesis: If it is better to dive to the bag, more players should dive. Right?

Well, ESPN's *Sports Science* program put that hypothesis to the test. The scientists on the show measured the overall speed of a runner who goes through the bag. They compared it to the overall speed of a runner who dives at the base. They measured acceleration versus deceleration—that is, increasing speed or decreasing speed.

Their simple experiment determined that when a player dives, he gets to the base

Safe! This player ran through first base instead of diving and turned a possible out into a hit.

10 milliseconds SLOWER than he gets there by running. He gets to first base faster by keeping his feet on the ground.

The conclusion: It's better to run *through* the bag.

As the show's host John Brenkus says, over the span of the 90 feet from home plate to first base, the 10 milliseconds that a fast player loses by diving at the bag (he loses even more if he dives too early and slides into the bag) "equates to about three inches—the diameter of baseball." On a bang-bang play at first, that tiny amount could be the difference between out and safe. For decades, coaches and fans have debated the dive versus. the run. Science says: The dive is . . . out!

Home on the Range

GLADWELL WOULD ARGUE THAT SUCCESS IN SPORTS is not just a matter of physical ability, but repetition. That repetition has to be targeted and correct, of course, or it won't do any good. A golfer can go to the practice range every day, but if he's practicing the

Backspin

One of the biggest differences between the PGA golfers and the everyday **hacker** on a public course is the pro's ability to stop his approach shot on the green by using backspin. That's especially helpful when a flag is placed in the front of the green, or near water or a sand trap, or when running the ball up to the hole is not an option. Some golfers, like Phil Mickelson, hit shots that can back up 10 or 20 feet toward the flagstick if conditions are right. It's almost as if they are pulling the ball back on a string!

A golfer gets backspin on the ball because of the friction that is produced when the club hits the ball. The club head has small grooves, or lines in it. The ball compresses slightly into the grooves—it can't be seen with the naked eye—and slides up the face of the club, which makes the ball spin backward. Any grass between the ball club and the ball will make it harder to spin and harder to control. That's why all golfers want to avoid the long grass called the rough, and keep it on the short grass called the fairway.

same things *wrong* over and over, he'll never improve his score.

That's where science comes in. From equipment design to course building to swing analysis and even to weather prediction, science has long played a part in the evolution of golf.

At first glance, playing golf for money looks like the easy life. After all, what could be nicer than playing 18 holes in four or five hours and then having the rest of the day off? But the reality is, most professional golfers go straight from the practice range to the course . . . and then back again. They are constantly trying to get the tiniest edge possible in an intense field in which everyone competes at an incredibly high level. Vijay Singh, a Fijian golfer who has won 34 tournaments on the Professional Golfers Association (PGA) Tour, is known for his legendary work ethic. He spends hours and hours on the range. He's not alone.

Actually, no golfer is alone on the range anymore. These days, a pro golfer is joined in his practice sessions not only by his caddie, but often also by a swing coach, a computer expert, and assorted other assistants to operate video cameras and provide immediate data analysis on the physics of his swing.

Perhaps the most important factor in the distance a golfer hits the ball is the amount

of **torque** that he generates. Torque is the turning force that produces rotation. You put torque on a toy top when you cause it to spin.

Cameras can slow down a golfer's swing to milliseconds so analysts can determine if he is generating enough torque to drive the ball down the fairway. They also measure his club-head speed, swing speed, shoulder turn, and more. Computer programs can put that data together to help a golfer and his coach make physical adjustments. The computer can then test those adjustments, too.

There is no secret to a perfect swing, Hall of Fame golfer-turned-television broadcaster Johnny Miller once told *Golf Digest* magazine.

The swing coach uses his expertise and video study to help a golfer create just the right amount of torque for his swing.

Rather, it's a matter of "coordinating physical movements so they can control the ball's flight."

Because no two swings are alike, the data is measured and analyzed to determine cause and effect for each individual golfer. Science says: Fore!

Medical Marvels

ONE OF THE MOST OBVIOUS EXAMPLES OF THE IMPACT science has had on athletes is in the area of sports medicine. For example, knee injuries once wiped out many football players' careers. Today, those knees can be fixed with arthroscopic surgery. For a baseball player, an elbow injury meant a pitcher would never see the mound again. Now such an injury is just a minor pothole on the road to stardom.

Thin steel instruments like these have revolutionized how medical scientists diagnose and treat joint injuries.

Arthroscopic surgery is almost considered routine these days, but it's an amazing scientific advancement. In the procedure, a surgeon makes a small incision in the skin instead of the large opening needed for regular surgery. Then, the doctor inserts an instrument about the size of a pencil.

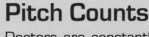

Pitch Counts

Doctors are constantly studying the reasons behind pitchers' injuries. Throwing a baseball overhand is an unnatural motion. Pitchers already are susceptible to injury. (For example, few women's softball pitchers, who throw with just as much force but in a more natural underhand motion, suffer arm injuries.)

A generation or so ago, the main culprit for injuries was believed to be throwing pitches such as the curveball at too early an age, before the arm had developed. Today, scientists believe that a greater concern for parents and youth coaches is overuse. For the most part, the more a pitcher throws at a young age, the more likely he is to need Tommy John surgery (page 18) later on. That's why there was a huge outcry when a prep pitcher in Florida threw 174 pitches in an extra-inning high school game in 2014.

Many youth coaches and leagues have taken the data presented by researchers and put limits to the number of pitches or innings thrown by their pitchers.

The instrument has a small lens and a lighting system that transmits video to a screen in the operating room. For a knee injury, the doctor can see if the cartilage or tendons are damaged, and he can look under the kneecap.

Flexible fiber optics in the 1970s helped make this surgery possible. But newer developments have made many more surgeries possible. Plus, according to the American Academy of Orthopaedic Surgeons (AAOS), many patients don't even need pain medica-

Thanks to Tommy John elbow surgery, Washington's Stephen Strasburg bounced back to top form.

tion afterwards. Athletes might be back in training in just a few weeks.

The recovery time is a lot longer for a baseball pitcher who needs what has come to be called "Tommy John surgery." Still, elbow reconstruction no longer is a career-ender. The surgery is named after left-hander Tommy John, who was one of the best pitchers in baseball for the Los Angeles Dodgers in the mid-1970s until the ulnar collateral ligament in his left arm gave way in 1974.

Dr. Frank Jobe, the team physician, tried a revolutionary new surgery. He took a tendon from a forearm or below the knee and weaved it into a figure-eight pattern. Then he threaded it through new holes drilled into the elbow bones. Jobe figured John had a one percent chance of returning to the big leagues. After one year of **rehabilitation**, John not only came back, but he went on to pitch in the Majors until 1989, when he was 46 years old. His 288 career victories rank seventh among left-handers in big-league history.

By the end of his career, John was a soft-toss pitcher who rarely struck anybody out. But he was never a hard thrower, anyway, even before his injury. He was a crafty pitcher who kept the ball down and relied on his fielders. In recent years, though, a number of hard-throwing strikeout pitchers, such as the Washington Nationals' Stephen Strasburg and the St. Louis Cardinals' Adam Wainwright, have bounced back from Tommy John surgery to become as good as new.

An unusually high number of big-league pitchers, including budding superstar Jose Fernandez of the Miami Marlins, underwent Tommy John surgery in 2014. That prompted a lot of worry among executives, fans, and the media over the cause of all the injuries. But the answer might be there are more surgeries because they are more successful. Elbow injuries simply don't mean the end of a pitcher's career anymore. It's hard work making it back, but studies show that from 74 to 92 percent of Tommy John surgeries are successful.

Science has provided a fix, and players are using it. Play on!

Advances in Prosthetics

IN 1984, AN AMERICAN BIOMEDICAL ENGINEER NAMED Van Phillips invented a **prosthetic** device for amputees called Flex-Foot. Phillips is an amputee himself. He lost a leg below the knee in a water-skiing accident when he was in college. He wanted to create a device that would allow amputees to do athletic things, such as running, as naturally as possible.

With prosthetics, athletes can accomplish nearly everything able-bodied people can manage . . . or more.

After creating Flex-Foot, Phillips continued to improve and innovate prosthetics. In 2012, his carbon-fiber prosthetics (carbon fiber is an amazingly strong, but light, man-made material) were used in the Summer Olympic Games in London in 2012 by South African sprinter Oscar Pistorius. Pistorius had both of his legs amputated below the knee when he was 11 months old because of a disease he was born with.

Phillips called the C-shaped prosthetics designed for elite athletes the Cheetah. "The Cheetah may be more [useful] than the human foot," Phillips once told the *New York Times*. "Carbon fiber graphite may be more energy efficient."

And there's the problem. Pistorius' entry

into the Olympic Games generated controversy over whether such a device should be allowed. As unthinkable as it sounds, did a physically challenged athlete have an advantage because of a prosthetic device? In the end, Pistorius was allowed to run, although he did not make the finals in his individual event, the 400 meters.

[Ed. Note: Pistorius' personal story took a tragic turn when he was accused of murdering his girlfriend in 2013. Before that, he was an inspiration to physically challenged athletes all over the world.]

Phillips' invention continues to make inroads. Though he has since sold the company, an estimated 90 percent of Paralympics athletes—the Paralympics are the Olympics for physically challenged athletes—use some variation of his original design.

TEXT-DEPENDENT QUESTIONS

1. Who was the doctor who invented the Tommy John surgery for elbows?
2. How do golfers use backspin in their shots to the green?
3. What is the name of the process scientists use to find answers?

RESEARCH PROJECTS

Compare Tommy John's career pitching statistics prior to his elbow injury in 1974 with his post-operation statistics. Would you say the operation was a success?

CHAPTER 2

TEAMS

Old-time football teams would be shocked to see such healthy food on their training table. But nutrition science is now helping teams make healthier choices.

THE TRADITIONAL IMAGE OF A FOOTBALL TRAINing table features 300-pound offensive linemen gorging themselves on inch-thick steaks and baked potatoes piled high with butter and sour cream. Those are washed down with sodas and followed by a dessert with brownies, pie, and ice cream. That training table is still an important way for some athletes to bulk up, and teams and college sports programs provide food for their athletes. However, at every level, today's sports teams are much more health conscious than they ever were before. The science of sports nutrition is just one way that teams are using science to help them win.

The New Training Table

THE FUNDAMENTALS OF SPORTS NUTRITION ARE SIMilar for all athletes, but the emphasis shifts according to need. The basics focus on hydration, calorie intake, protein, and vitamins and minerals. For instance, a cross-country skier at the Winter Olympics needs to maximize her endurance levels. An ice hockey player might be more interested in power and speed. Most teams use sports nutritionists to help plan meals. These experts have studied the science behind food, and can properly balance intake levels to meet the athletes' needs.

The U.S. Men's National Soccer Team that competed at the World Cup in Brazil in 2014 traveled with two full-time chefs, as well as a nutrition consultant. The "food team" prepared meals every day the team was on the road. They timed the meals to help players recover from games or practices or to help them deal with extreme weather conditions. Among the many items players found were dried cherries, peanut butter balls, and protein shakes. What they didn't find: soda, chips, or fatty foods. In fact, avocados were shipped by the crateful to Brazil to give the team "good fat." As team nutritionist Danielle LaFata told *Sports Illustrated*, the goal is "teaching guys to view food as an energy source for performance and recovery."

WORDS TO UNDERSTAND

electrolyte a substance necessary for a body to use nutrition properly; often lost during heavy athletic workouts.

dehydration a state of being in which a body is lacking water or important fluids.

Science has proven to players what they should have heard from their parents: Eating right is the best way to succeed. However, food science has taken that many steps further, providing teams and players with individual meal plans tailored specifically to each athlete and each sport.

Naming Rights

THE MORE TEAMS UNDERSTAND ABOUT FATIGUE AND dehydration, the more they can adapt and maximize performance from their athletes. One of the most famous historical examples of this led to the invention of Gatorade.

Whether you play at home or in a packed stadium, nothing is more important than staying hydrated.

In 1965, a University of Florida assistant football coach went to medical researchers at the school. He wanted help avoiding dehydration in the hot weather of training camp. Dr. Robert Cade and his team of physicians went into the lab and began experimenting. Eventually, they produced, as Gatorade's web

Sticky Shower

Keeping its players hydrated is important for any sports team. In general, the best way is the most natural way: water. But during competition, sports drinks such as Gatorade are helpful for replacing lost electrolytes . . . and for dousing coaches with a sticky shower after a big win!

The tradition of the Gatorade shower generally is credited to the New York Giants in the 1986 season. That year, star defensive lineman Jim Burt first doused head coach Bill Parcells as a prank following one of the Giants' victories, in revenge for some verbal abuse Burt took during the week leading

up to the game. Pro Football Hall of Fame linebacker Harry Carson took it from there, orchestrating a Gatorade shower for Parcells after each of the team's victories through Super Bowl XXI that season.

site says, a "precisely balanced carbohydrate-**electrolyte** beverage that would adequately replace the key components lost by Gator players through sweating and exercise." Naturally, it was known as . . . "Cade's Ade." Later, it was named Gatorade after the nickname of the university's sports teams.

Today, the Gatorade Sports Science Institute in Barrington, Ill., and its satellite lab in the warmer-weather clime of Bradenton, Fla., continue to research the effects of exercise and nutrition on the human body. Its labs study physiology, biochemistry, body composition, exercise performance, and more.

From the Land Down Under

USUALLY WHEN SPORTS teams and leagues are on the cutting edge of science and technology, they are happily eager to talk about it on social media and in traditional media. They want to attract fans, recruits, or potential

Australian Rules Football players benefit from **GPS** info gathered by the black vest shown here.

signees. That's not always the case with teams that use Catapult Sports. In fact, the Australia-based company bills itself as "The Most-Used Secret in Sport." Maybe that's because teams don't want others to think they're gaining an unfair competitive advantage. Or maybe it's because the science behind the technology is so new that they don't want others to learn from how they've adapted.

Catapult outfits athletes with GPS (Global Positioning System) devices attached to a type of harness they wear at practice. Even though the harnesses look like sports bras, it's important that the devices are as unobtrusive as possible so they don't affect performance.

The GPS devices measure dozens of data points, including things such as speed, distance acceleration, heart rate, workload, and

Coaches can monitor their athletes' movements in real time during practice sessions.

more. By monitoring such data, the theory goes, coaches can maintain an optimum performance level for their players. They can prevent overwork or fatigue, which leads to injuries like muscle tears or hamstring pulls.

Catapult's product sounds like something straight out of the future. Only the future is now for teams in sports and leagues from Australia Rules Football to rugby to soccer to college and pro football, and more.

One of the college football teams that uses Catapult Sports is Florida State University, which went undefeated and won the national championship for 2013. Head coach Jimbo Fisher is quick to credit Catapult for helping the Seminoles make the leap to the top of the college football world. He believes the

The Catapult device creates charts, graphs, and reports for coaches and athletes to study.

technology helped the team cut way down on injuries, keeping its best players on the field more often.

Of course, all raw data the GPS collects doesn't mean a thing if teams don't know what to do with it. So at Florida State, Fisher em-

Florida State football points to GPS tech as one of the reasons for its ongoing success.

ploys a former engineer at the Kennedy Space Center in Cape Canaveral to sort through the numbers in real time on the sidelines and to make recommendations. For instance, the data once revealed that a star wide receiver's performance sometimes dropped off because too often the coaches had him demonstrate the right way to do things to the other receivers on the team. The coaches adjusted accordingly, and cut back the player's workload.

Right now, the GPS technology isn't allowed during games. But that could change one day. So far, Catapult's clients include more than a dozen NFL teams. Other college teams that use the product include Baylor University, whose athletic department includes an "Applied Performance" department, and Louisiana State University.

LSU strength coach Tommy Moffitt told CBS Sports that GPS conditioning "is to strength and conditioning what the barbell was forty or fifty years ago."

TEXT-DEPENDENT QUESTIONS

1. What are some of the key changes in teams' approach to nutrition?
2. What problem do sports drinks like Gatorade try to overcome?
3. How do Catapult products capture information about player movement?

RESEARCH PROJECTS

Go online and find other articles or stories about pro and college teams using data-capture devices like Catapult. Think about what you would learn if you wore such a device while you played your favorite sport.

CHAPTER 3

ARENAS, FIELDS, AND FANS

REMEMBER WHEN AN OVERHEAD CAMERA VIEW from the blimp was a big deal? Okay, maybe that's before your time. How about when the yellow first-down line first appeared on the television screen for football games? Or when instant-replay first was used to help officials?

Today, science has helped create technoology that helps officials (and television viewers) determine if a goal is scored in soccer, if a baseball is a home run, if a judges' line call is correct in tennis, and if the shooter got his last-second three-pointer off in time in basketball. Advances in physics, computer science, and electronics have all played a part.

The NFL is one of several pro sports leagues around the world that use video replay technology.

Indeed, there are plenty of obvious technological advances in sports in recent years, especially visible when we watch competition on television from the comfort of our homes. But the science behind such technology also has contributed to on-field improvements. In fact, sporting venues all over the world turn to science to improve competition.

That's Racin'

WINNING A NASCAR OR FORMULA 1 RACE IS a lot more than a matter of going faster than anyone else and avoiding accidents. It takes a great deal of expertise in negotiating turns on the oval track . . . and a little knowledge of science helps. Or, as physics professor Leslie Pelecky of the University of Texas at Dallas says, "you need the right science to turn left."

Just about everyone in racing starts a race with an excellent car. And every driver has to be a great one to reach that elite level. So the drivers that can best negotiate the turns on the track are the most successful.

Centripetal force (see page 36) is what keeps a race car going in a circular motion around the track. But it takes thousands of pounds of centripetal force—more than two tons, in fact—to keep the car from flying into the wall.

Drivers need to know the precise moment

when to back off the speed going into a turn, and when to accelerate out of the turn to maintain the proper force in the small part of the car—the tires—that is in contact with the road. Think what would happen if you were performing "Around the World" with a yo-yo and suddenly let go of the string. Or if you didn't let go, but released the tension in the string.

Scientists and engineers study those forces when designing the cars. They have to take into account the weight of the car and the speed it is going. The exterior of the car also needs to be aerodynamic; that is, it needs to let the air slip over it at high speed without slowing the car. NASCAR's current "Generation 6" cars

The high banks of a race track help the driver counter-act the forces that are trying to wreck his car.

Centripetal Force

Centripetal (senn-TRIP-ih-tul) force is the force necessary to keep an object moving in a curved path, as in a circle. It is a forced directed inward, toward the center of the circle. That's compared to the centrifugal (senn-TRIH-fih-gul) force, which is a force pushing an object away from the center.

are now the standard for each team, though each team adds its own design changes depending on which car company sponsors it. The cars also have on-board computers that send streams of data back to pit crews and team technicians. That data is analyzed during and after each race to show where the design worked . . . and where it didn't. Formula 1 cars also use **telemetry** to send a constant stream of data to their teams. Using scientific models, the teams analyze the data for ways to improve their racing machines.

During a race, however, drivers don't have time for science. They just have to know that a steep-banked track like the one at Dover International Speedway in Delaware lets them take turns at faster speed than the flatter track at Phoenix International Raceway in Arizona. It's in the turns that they generate the momentum they need to pass other cars on the straightaway and take the checkered flag. But the ability of their car to make those turns and passes starts in the mind of an engineer and in the science of physics.

Cool Design

WHEN BRAZIL WON THE BID TO HOST THE 2014 World Cup, it knew it would have to build new stadiums and improve existing ones. Some stadiums were renovated with better irrigation or lighting systems (see page 38). A $450-million stadium called Are-

Arena das Dunas in Natal, Brazil, used high-tech design to make fans comfortable.

na das Dunas ("The Stadium of the Dunes") was built in Natal.

The distinctive "petal" shape of the Arena das Dunas' roof tiles is not just a to make it look pretty. True, the wavy exterior looks like nearby sand dunes, but architects Christopher Lee and Dave Orlowski relied on **fluid dynamics** to give the form function. Fluid

Bright Lights, Big City

If you watched soccer's World Cup on television in the summer of 2014, you were probably amazed at how green the grass looked. Did you see the bright colors at the old Maracana stadium in Rio de Janeiro? You can thank the maintenance crews and World Cup organizers for an amazing job. But give credit also to the scientists who studied and adjusted the stadium lights. According to ESPN's *Sports Science*, each of the nearly 400 floodlights in the stadium was positioned at just the right height, just the right angle, and just far enough apart to provide uniform lighting throughout the pitch. Any variations in lighting were so minor that they couldn't be detected without sophisticated equipment.

dynamics is the science of how air or liquid moves over a surface. By knowing how the wind will pass over a building, designers can use that wind to their advantage.

At Arena das Dunas, the petals of the roof tiles are spaced apart and rise higher on one

side of the stadium than the other in order. They let just the right amount of wind to pass through, circulate, and help cool fans in the stands and players on the field in the hot and humid climate.

On free kicks in soccer, the defense can set a wall **10** yards away from the spot of the kick.

Do Not Cross!

WHEN ONE TEAM IS AWARDED A FREE KICK, direct or indirect, in soccer, the players on the opposing team are required to stand at least 10 yards (9.15 meters) away from the ball. It's a time-honored

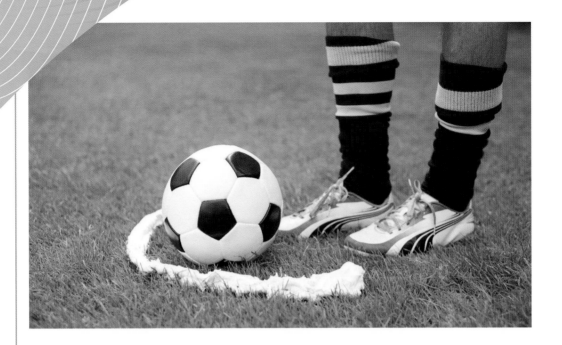

The disappearing foam circle makes sure the kicking team does not gain an advantage by moving the ball closer to goal.

tradition in soccer, though, that after the referee has stepped off the yardage, defenders creep forward. The referee pushes them back . . . and they creep forward again. He pushes them back . . . and they creep forward again, until the ball is eventually kicked.

At the World Cup in 2014, science helped put an end to that game of cat-and-mouse. Each referee carried with him a small spray can. When the referee awarded a free kick, he sprayed a small semicircle of white foam at the point the kick was to be made. Then he stepped off 10 yards, and drew a line with the spray. That marked where the defenders had to stand. No more arguments!

The spray (it's called 9.15 Fair Play after the

distance from the kick as measured in meters) is a mixture of butane and other gases, combined with water, a foaming agent, and other chemicals. It had been used at soccer games around the world, including Major League Soccer matches in the United States, but 2014 marked the first time it had been used in the World Cup.

After about one minute, the foaming spray dissolves, leaving behind no visible line on the field—until the referee sprays again on the next foul.

Going Green

A GOLFER'S HOME FIELD IS THE golf course. One of the best things about playing golf is that it means hours and hours of fresh air playing outside and enjoying nature (hopefully enjoying the short grass of the fairways and not the trees near the out-of-bounds markers!).

The science of **agronomy** helps create the proper environment for the sport. Agronomy is an agricultural science that studies plants and the soil and how they interact, grow, and develop. In fact,

A lot of work and science goes into making sure that golf courses remain green.

a golf course is one big outdoor science lab. Course designers, superintendents, and their staffs need to make a wide range of science-based decisions. They consider environmental issues such as the right grass to use in different places; which plant life will work best; when and how much to irrigate; and how to care for the soil in which the grass is growing. They also have to take into account issues relating to how the game is played, such as the speed of the putting greens and the slope of the course.

The right choices not only mean a better

Making sure a golf course stays beautiful takes hours of mowing and careful choices by scientifcally trained experts.

place to play for golfers, but also make a positive environmental impact. The United States Golf Association (USGA) has a long list of ideas for golf course designers to help them make eco-friendly courses. Those ideas include not using pesticides, choosing drought-tolerant grass, and choosing sites that don't need as much earth moved to create them. They even write about ways that course owners should treat animals that live on the courses, even if they are animals such as skunks that they don't want to live there!

Wherever sports are played, science is playing a bigger and bigger part in creating the fields, arenas, and parks of the world.

TEXT-DEPENDENT QUESTIONS

1. *What was the science used in designing Arena das Dunas in Brazil?*
2. *What is the force that keeps race cars moving in a curved path?*
3. *What is soccer's disappearing foam made from?*

RESEARCH PROJECTS

Roll a tennis ball on a flat surface. Does the ball tend to move in a straight line? What forces might make it deviate from a straight line? Now roll the ball at the same speed on a banked surface? Does it still move in a straight line?

CHAPTER 4

GEAR

Science is helping to make safety gear like pads and helmets worn by football players lighter and safer.

WHEN IT COMES TO THE GEAR THAT ATH-letes use, science means safety. More than ever before, scientists, researchers, and engineers are helping create gear that keeps athletes safer than ever before. Experts study the motions, power, strength, and energy of athletes, especially related to the collisions between them. They combine that knowledge with stronger but lighter-weight materials to make protective gear. Players in contact sports are bigger and faster than ever.

The science of physics tells us that the force, or power, of a collision is equal to the mass (or weight) times the speed (also known as acceleration). Scientists write that equation as $F = mA$. Athletes can wear sensors that give scientists the speed and force data to plug into that and other equations. What comes out the other end might help prevent injuries . . . or even save lives.

Perhaps the most important area of athlete safety relates to concussions. A concussion occurs when the head suffers a blow that moves the brain around inside the skull. They can be very dangerous to a person's long-term health. Some happen at once with a single blow. Other smaller concussions can build up over time to affect a person. Because of all that, the study of concussions is a major part of every contact sport these days. And the number-one such sport is football. According to the United States Centers for Disease Control and Prevention (CDC), there may be as many as 3.8 million sports-related concussions in America each year. Football, with violent collisions on the scale of a car accident on every play, is perhaps the most visible contributor to that number. The efforts of science to help players stay safe starts at the top.

Helmets: More Than Just Hard Hats

HELMETS HAVE COME A LONG WAY FROM THE ORIGInal leather headgear developed in the late 19th century. The first football

WORDS TO UNDERSTAND

aerodynamic the science of how air moves and how objects move through it

compresses reduces in size

coefficient of restitution the measurement of how much a surface rebounds after it is compressed

dimples on a golf ball, the tiny indentations that cover the surface

players could fold up their "helmets" and put them in a pocket. Plastic helmets were finally used after World War II. Facemasks were added in the 1950s. Today's helmets are the result of research and study to make better headgear for players in several sports.

Energy, force, and momentum are all physics concepts in play on every football tackle. The energy of a fast-moving athlete colliding with another fast-moving (and heavy) player creates great force. If that force cannot be reduced by pads and helmets, it can cause great damage to a person's body. A 300-pound defensive lineman can put out a lot of force!

On both sides of such a collision, players wear helmets made of molded plastic with foam-rubber pads inside. Helmets also have inflatable air pads. The pads are blown up using a special pump to ensure that each helmet perfectly fits the wearer. The helmets are also designed so that the padding **compresses** when a player is struck, lessening the average

The hard outer shell of a helmet spreads out the impact; interior padding also protects the skull.

force of the blow. The helmet's shell distributes the force over a wider area. Shoulder pads and other protective equipment work much the same way.

Research is being done to learn even more. Sensors can be attached to helmets to measure the forces exactly. Some systems can even relay data wirelessly to a sideline monitor. A team doctor can alert the coaches to remove a player who has received a signficantly hard hit.

What about other sports? Major League Baseball players wear helmets when batting. Many youth leagues now make batters wear facemasks *and* helmets. Pitchers are vulnerable to being hit, too. In 2014, Tampa Bay pitcher Alex Torres was the first to use a specially padded cap while pitching. Given its large size, it won't catch on, but researchers are still looking for a smaller, safer way. Even base coaches now wear protective helmets.

The National Hockey League's players all wear helmets and most also wear faceguards. Their body pads have become much lighter, allowing for faster skating . . . and harder collisions. Overall, science and engineering have made every collision sport safer, but there is still more work to do.

In lacrosse, Irish hurling, and even hard-hitting rugby, other protective padding is being used to reduce injuries.

Helmet History

Here's some great football trivia for you. The NFL began play in 1920 (it was called the American Professional Football Association back then). However, helmets have been mandatory only since 1943.

Baseball helmets have been a permanent part of the game since 1970. Boston Red Sox catcher Bob Montgomery, who retired in 1979, was the last player allowed to play without one.

The National Hockey League didn't force players to wear helmets until 1979. It also let players who already had signed a pro contract go without one. That meant that as late as 1997, an NHL player (the St. Louis Blues' Craig MacTavish) went helmetless.

And what about goalie masks? It might surprise you to know that pro ice hockey was played for more than 70 years before goalies started wearing masks regularly. Talk about looking for trouble!

It's All in the Stitching

EVER WONDER WHY A MAJOR LEAGUE BASEBALL pitcher sometimes throws back a brand-new baseball to the umpire? Sometimes, the pitcher will even throw a second one back, too. Well, there's a reason pitchers are so particular, and it's the obvious one: The baseballs just don't *feel* right. Because baseballs are hand-stitched, the stitching on each ball isn't always exactly the same. The seams that hold the two pieces of leather together can be a bit different. Those seams on a

To throw a curve-ball, a pitcher pushes against the raised seams on the ball and turns his wrist as he releases the pitch.

Major League baseball rise about 0.5 millimeters above the surface of the ball. If they're too high, the ball might do some crazy things and be harder to control. If they are too low, and the ball might be harder to spin, and just sit right over the plate for the batter to crush. But without any seams at all, baseballs would not always go straight. Pitchers push on the seams with their fingers to create rotation, along with turning their wrists to create various kinds of spin. All those various rotations can make a ball move in flight by creating different types of momentum. Thanks to physics and stitches (and pitchers' skill!), baseballs really can curve.

Thwack! Ping?

FOR MANY YEARS, HIGH SCHOOLS AND COLLEGES used the same wood bats used in pro baseball. Those bats, however, are expensive and break often. So in the 1970s, schools began using bats made of aluminum. The familiar (and comfortable) *thwack* of ball on wood was replaced by the *ping* of ball on aluminum.

The change in bats also brought with it a scientific idea called "**coefficient of restitution**" (COR). The not-so-technical definition of COR is . . . bounciness.

At the moment the baseball makes contact with the bat, the ball is compressed. With hard, wood bats, the ball is compressed more, and it takes more force by the swinger to make the ball go far. With hollow aluminum

COR

Coefficient of restitution is based on a mathematical formula developed by Sir Isaac Newton in the 17th century. COR is represented by a number between 0 and 1, in which 0 is completely inelastic (no bounciness at all between two objects at a collision) and 1 is very elastic. Newer synthetic bats must have a certified coefficient of restitution of .5 or less.

This aluminum bat will compress when the ball hits it. Springing back then gives the ball extra force.

bats, the "walls" of the bat give in slightly. The ball is not compressed as much. The ball retains its pitched energy, and it doesn't take as much force from the bat to make the ball go far. Think of jumping on a trampoline as opposed to jumping on concrete, or bouncing a basketball off the hardwood as opposed to a grass field. With an aluminum bat, the ball is bouncing off a trampoline!

Researchers found that the COR on aluminum bats was far greater than that on wood bats. But it didn't take a scientist to see that! Fans and players could see that balls flew off the aluminum bats.

College players began hitting home runs in record numbers. Games were longer, and scores were much higher. It got so ridiculous that in 1999, the University of Southern

California won the national championship by beating Arizona State by a score of 21–14 in the title game.

Bats with a high COR were creating a safety hazard, too. College baseball officials wanted to be sure they did something before a pitcher or infielder was unable to react in time to the line drives flying off the aluminum bats. Youth league officials worried about the bats as well; even kids can hit hard line drives with aluminum bats.

So beginning in 2011, college baseball required bats to have a coefficient of restitution of no more than 0.5 (see box on page 51). The new bats, called BBCOR ("Bat-Ball Coefficient of Restitution") worked—but just a little

The Brazuca

The World Cup soccer ball for 2014 had panels just as previous balls had. Extensive **aerodynamic** lab testing—not to mention on-field play in 30 countries—showed that the new six-panel "Brazuca" ball sailed truer than ever. It was better than the eight-paneled 2010 ball or the 14-paneled 2006 ball. The Brazuca also had a new surface structure that featured thousands of tiny bumps. FIFA (soccer's international governing body) promised "improved grip, touch, stability, and aerodynamics on the pitch."

For the first time, too, the panels on the 2014 ball were pieced together by thermal bonding instead of stitching. No stitching meant no seams, and no seams meant less water retention in rainy weather in Brazil.

When college baseball went to a CCOR bat, home runs became rare, but hitters adjusted quickly.

too well! Scoring plummeted, and home runs became rare. That meant another adjustment . . . in the height of the seams allowed on a college ball. Lowering the seams means less drag on a batted ball, helping it to fly further. In lab tests, the NCAA determined that for a typical home-run swing, the ball traveled 20 feet farther with lowered seams. The lower the seams, too, the less break on a pitcher's curveball, giving hitters a better chance at making contact. Science is the middle of a battle for the best possible baseball action.

That change was in place for 2015, and officials planned to monitor the statistics to see if the change had the desired effect.

Why Dimples?

I**T TAKES ONLY ONE LOOK AT A GOLF BALL TO SEE THAT** it's not like any other ball in sports. A golf ball is not smooth, or pebbled, or paneled. Instead, it has unique dents covering its surface. Those dents, called **dimples**, aren't for looks. They are designed to reduce drag.

Drag is basically a fancy way of saying wind resistance. (Or, more precisely, air resistance, since drag can be a factor even if there's no wind.) If a golf ball was smooth—and the original ones were—the air resistance would be greater and would cut down on how far the ball can fly through the air. The dimples on

Aerodynamics

Aerodynamics is the science that studies the movement of air and how objects move through it. It plays a big part in many, many sports.

A football quarterback is familiar with aerodynamics because he knows a tight spiral cuts through the air with less resistance and is more likely to reach its target than a wobbly throw that is more susceptible to the forces around it.

A race-car driver knows that he can "draft" the driver in front, staying close to his bumper to create a vacuum that makes both cars go faster—until he decides to break the vacuum and "slingshot" past.

And a skateboarder knows that she wants to crouch down on her board for a smaller profile that makes for less resistance against the air.

the golf ball redirect the air flow by creating peaks and valleys for it to travel over. That allows a dimpled ball to travel nearly twice as far as a ball without dimples.

The (USGA) doesn't regulate the number of dimples or the size of the dimples on a golf ball. But scientists at the USGA do constantly

Golf balls are made with dimples to create straight and true shots . . . if the golfer knows what he's doing!

test the effects of dimples on a golf ball. Golf ball makers are doing research as well. It's a constant battle to find the pattern of dimples that sends a ball flying straightest and farthest. In this case, science can turn into millions of dollars for the companies that discover the best patterns.

TEXT-DEPENDENT QUESTIONS

1. What determines the amount of force that occurs in an impact?

2. Why did college baseball teams switch to BBCOR bats?

3. How do dimples help a golf ball fly straight?

RESEARCH PROJECTS

Head out to a park with some friends and kick a soccer ball around. How can you make the ball curve, or bend? What happens when you kick the top half of the ball? The bottom half? What about the right side? The left side?

WINNING . . . AND THE FUTURE

CHAPTER 5

ODAY, EVERY MAJOR LEAGUE BASE-ball team has at least dipped its toes into the statistical analysis pool called Sabermetrics. (The name originates from SABR, the Society for American Baseball Research.) Sabermetrics is a way to judge athletes with hard data more than just with human judgment. Some clubs have done more than dip their toes into Sabermetrics, they've dived right in. In the late 1990s and early 2000s, Oakland and its general manager Billy Beane remade their teams with such stats. Michael Lewis' 2003 best-selling book *Moneyball* and a movie made from the book told that story. In today's game, the Houston Astros have a director of decision sciences who has two engineering degrees and has worked for NASA.

Beane's success in Oakland started a war between the new generation of Sabermetricians and old-school baseball scouts. Today, the war is over, as big-league teams combine the old and new approaches while using the best of each.

That's a good comparison for what's happening with science and sports in general. There's a fine line between using scientific advances and misusing them. Unfortunately, in some cases, people have misused science with the rise of performance-enhancing drugs in sports. The use of PEDs, or "doping," is the dark side of scientific advances in sports.

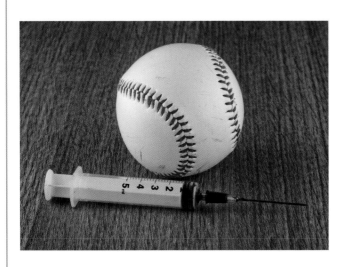

PEDs include many products taken by athletes to improve performance. They can include human-growth hormone (HGH) and stimulants. The most obvious example came in baseball's Steroid Era of the late 1990s and early 2000s. It wasn't until 2002 that baseball banned steroids and began imposing stiff penalties for its use. Steroid use has

The Steroid Era was a black time for baseball, as many records and stars were called into question.

tainted the achievements of many players of the era, including slugger Barry Bonds. Even though he is baseball's all-time home-run king, Bonds is widely viewed as a product of the Steroid Era and is not in the National Baseball Hall of Fame.

Athletes in other sports, too, have come under the PED microscope, most notably biker Lance Armstrong, who had his seven consecutive Tour de France titles from 1999 to 2005 stripped for doping.

But while scientific advances helped some athletes to cheat, advances in science are also combating that kind of cheating with more efficient testing methods. That's not only good for athletes, who know it's a level playing field for everyone, but for fans, too, who know they are watching a fair fight.

Fair is at the center of all sporting competitions. Can science tip the balance of fairness in sports? At what point does science take over and make games not games anymore?

Science can hurt, but it is mostly helping in sports. That is also part of the nature of athletics. No matter how much science (or technology, engineering, or math) plays a role, it is still a person who has to put the ball in the hole . . . or race across the finish line . . . or kick the ball into the back of the net.

And that will never change.

FURTHER RESOURCES

Books

TIME for Kids: Amazing Sports and Science
By the editors of Time for Kids Magazine
Time Home Entertainment Inc., 2014

Gold Medal Physics: The Science of Sports
By John Eric Goff
Johns Hopkins University Press, 2010
(Note: Available as Kindle e-book)

Why a Curveball Curves: The Incredible Science of Sports
By Frank Vizard
Hearst Books, 2009

Runner's World Presents: The Runner's Body—How the Latest Exercise Science Can Help You Run Stronger, Longer, Faster
By Ross Tucker, Jonathan Dugas, and Matt Fitzgerald
Rodale, 2011

Web Sites

espn.go.com/sportscience
Videos from the TV show, which also appear as segments on SportsCenter, show many ways that science can be used to explain and explore sports of all kinds.

popularmechanics.com/outdoors/sports/
Popular Mechanics, one of the world's best magazines for hands-on science has a section of its site devoted to sports technology and science.

exploratorium.edu/explore/staff_picks/sports_science/
The amazing Exploratorium science museum in San Francisco posts this page with stories about science and baseball, skateboarding, hockey, and more.

SERIES GLOSSARY: WORDS TO UNDERSTAND

aerodynamic The science of how air moves and how objects move through it

applications In this case, ways of using information in a specific way to find answers

carbon fiber A material woven of carbon atoms that offers a wide range of high-strength and high-flexibility properties

cognitive training Software and hardware that trains the brain and the body's senses.

fluid dynamics The science of how air or liquid moves over a surface

GPS: Global positioning system Technology that bounces a signal off satellites to pinpoint the exact location of where the signal originated from

logistics The science of organizing large numbers of people, materials, or events

parabola A symmetrical curved path. In stadiums, a roof overhang can create a parabola by bouncing noise from below back down toward the field of play

prosthetics Devices that replace a missing human limb

prototype A model of a future product made to test design and engineering issues

rehabilitation The process of returning to full physical ability through exercise

velocity Measurement of the speed of an object

ventilation The easy movement of air around or within a body or a system

INDEX

Photo Credits

Front cover: DollarPhotoClub/Snaptitude
Interior Images: *Courtesy of Catapult Sports:* 27, 28, 29; *DollarPhotoClub:* WayneG 50, Koufax73 60; *Dreamstime.com:* Nexusplexus 6; Arenacreative 8; Jamie Roach 12; Photogolfer 15; Wickedgood 18, 26; Srekap 20; Offscreen 22; Dirima 25; Ruth Peterkin 30; Walter Arce 35; Marchello 74 37; MaxiSports 39; Konart 40; Daniel Thornberg 41; Larry Jordan 42; Willeecole 47; Photographerlondon 52; Aspenphoto 54; Monika Wisniewska 56; Lawrence Weslowski Jr. 58; *Courtesy Lut Endoscopy:* 16; *Joe Robbins:* 32, 45
Backgrounds: Dreamstime.com/Shuttlecock (2)

About the Author

Jim Gigliotti has written more than 50 books on sports for young readers. He is a former senior editor at NFL Publishing, where he was on the team that started NFL.com as well as created weekly and annual programs for NFL teams and the league. His recent books include biographies of Edgar Allan Poe, Mother Teresa, and Bruce Lee.